The Viking Stone Age

Birth of the Ax Culture

by Njord Kane

GW00707706

Published on: November 1, 2016 by Spangenhelm Publishing

Interior Design and Cover by: Njord Kane

ISBN-13: 978-1-943066-20-9

ISBN-10: 1943066205

1. Vikings 2. Norse 3. Ancient History

First Edition.

10 9 8 7 6 5 4 3 2 1

iv

Table of Contents

Preface.....................................vii

Chapter 1 - Who were the Vikings?..... ....pg 5

Chapter 2 – The Nordic Stone Age..... .....pg 17

Chapter 3 – The Metallic Ages ....pg 41

References .... pg 55

Preface

This book is divided into two parts. The first part tells the Norse story chronologically from an anthropologist's point of view. Starting from the early Norse people during the Stone Age that migrated as hunter-gathers following herds of megafauna, such as Mammoths.

From the Stone Age into the gradual progression of settling and forming into a complex society. Detailing the steps of Norse society as they evolved into the far reaching "viking" explorers that changed and modified the World we know today.

The second part of this book highlights specifics about ancient Norse culture, technology, beliefs, and practices.

The Norse were a major indigenous people

of Scandinavia and Northern Europe. When we refer to them, we often see the words Vikings and Norse used interchangeably without discrimination. So which term is correct when referring to these people? Do we call them Vikings or Norse?

At first thought, we usually call them Vikings. This is because when we mention the Vikings, immediately everyone knows we're talking about the Norse.

However, the term "Viking" is not actually what the Norse people called themselves. It was actually something they did.

The word Viking comes from the Old Norse word "víkingr," a term which meant to go raiding and it wasn't always by boat. The word Viking was only later used to refer to the Norse people whom were conducting these raids.

There are a variety of other stereotypes commonly associated with "Vikings." Most are simply false stereotypes such as the horned or winged helmet for example.

Calling them "Vikings" is technically

incorrect. However it's of such common use today that when we call them Vikings, everyone knows that we're referring to the Norse. Even though Viking was something they did (raid) and not what they were called.. or how they referred to themselves. They were actually called the Norse or Northmen.

A statement of fact is: all Vikings were Norse, but not all Norse were Vikings. In fact, most Norse were farmers – just like everyone else on the planet during the time.

The purpose of this book is to provide a concise and up to date historical chronicle about the Norse people. With so many recent discoveries by archaeologists studying the Norse, there are many things that we had previously thought we knew about the Norse that has changed.

This makes the Nordic story as previously taught out of date and in need of being retold. This book tells the Norse story current to today's discoveries, presented in short chapters through each epoch of Nordic history.

We start our story about the Norse from

the first proof of existence as an identifiable and distinct people. A people whom migrated into Scandinavia and the Northern European area many thousands of years ago. We then take you through their progression from hunter-gathers into the agricultural settlements that eventually grew into societies.

A journey through the rise and expansion of Nordic culture that forever help form Europe and Western Culture as a whole. Highlighting new discoveries in Norse knowledge and technologies, that were previously a mystery to scientists.

This book is not the single work of the author, but the combined works of hundreds of years by thousands of researchers that have spent lifetimes trying to unravel the story and mystery of the Norse people.

There has been so many recent discoveries by modern researchers, the Nordic story has been rewritten from what we thought we used to know about their obscure history. A history that was almost lost in time and obscure mythology.

2

The Beginnings of a People

Chapter 1
Who were the Vikings?

The "Vikings" were an ancient people that inhabited Northern Europe and Scandinavia known as the Norse (also known as Northmen or Norsemen). The Norse people were spread across Northern Europe, particularly in the regions known today as: Scandinavia (Norway, Sweden, and Finland), Germany, Denmark, Poland, Netherlands, the United Kingdom (England, Scotland, Ireland, and the surrounding islands), Iceland, Russia, Latvia, Lithuania, and Estonia.

These northern people as a whole spoke as their native language, one the various dialects of Norse. The Norse language was a Northern Germanic / Scandinavian language that was in wide use before the Christianization of Northern Europe, Russia, and Scandinavia.

The Norse are today most commonly known to people as the "Vikings." However, the term "viking" was not actually what the Norse people called themselves. It was something that they did. The word "viking" comes from the Old Norse word "víkingr," a term which meant to go raiding for loot and it was something that wasn't always done by boat. A Viking was a Norse Raider.

The word viking was only later misused when referring to the Norse people as a whole, instead of just those specific Norsemen whom conducted the Viking raids. Simply put, a "Viking" is a raider, or more correctly; a Norseman whom went raiding. In more precise terms, a Viking is a Norse Raider.

With this in mind, we know that calling the Norse people "Vikings" as a whole is incorrect. However it is of such common use today that when someone calls them Vikings, everyone knows that they are talking about the Norse. Although, in most cases, they are referring to Norse Raiders, in which case, "Vikings" would be correct. But to reiterate, viking was something they did (raid) and the people were actually called the Norse.

A statement of fact is: **all Vikings were Norse, but not all Norse were Vikings**.

In fact, most Norse were farmers and tradesman – just like everyone else on the planet. I had said all of this in the preface of this book, but found it necessary to repeat myself because I simply can't stress this fact enough.

There are also many other misunderstandings and stereotypes that are commonly associated with the term "Viking." One of the most common false stereotypes about the Norse and especially of viking raiders is that of the horned or winged helmet for example.

The Norse never wore winged or horned helmets - that is fiction. The types of helmets the Norse wore is discussed further ahead in this book's chapter about Norse Arms and

Armor.

The winged and horned helmet were mistakenly used to depict Vikings in an opera. The opera singer's costumes of winged and horned helmets stuck as a common belief as to what the Norse used to look like and what they wore.

Statue of a Viking in Gimli, Manitoba (Canada).42

As glorious as many of these false depictions may be; such as horned helmets being a sort of universal icon as to identify Vikings.

We'll clear up these misconceptions as we go further along in the book and look closely at what the Norse really did and what they were really like. We'll look at the facts of what was real about the Norse people and their culture. We'll also look specifically at the Norse that infamously raided during the Viking Era, giving them the label as Vikings.

The history of the Norse people goes all the way back to the Stone Age, but they are best known for a period of time when they raided several parts of Europe known as the Viking Age.

The Viking Age is typically recorded in history as occurring approximately around 793 AD to 1066 AD. This period of time is not the time span of the Norse people themselves, nor was it the peak of their civilization. This is merely the height of the time when the Norse people were mostly written about. The time when they reached out and went out on viking adventures. A time when the World noticed them and were fearful.

The Viking Age began somewhere just before the date of 800 AD. The actual beginning of the Viking Age is a bit foggy and different locations argue different time periods of when viking raids actually began to occur.

To abolish this argument, it is generally accepted in the academic community that the official beginning of the Viking Age is to have begun on the 8th of June 793 AD. This date is when there is a formal recording made of when Norse Raiders (Vikings) made an attack on the monastery at Lindisfarne, an island off the northeast coast of England.

The attack came unexpected, as it was an unguarded religious community of Christian monks. An easy target for Vikings sailing around the coast in search of a place they can easily raid and loot.

The Viking raiders were seeking an easy target that was close to the water, so they didn't have to go far from their boats. The Norse preferred to raid near their boats to allow them a hasty escape before reinforcements could come.

Allowing the Vikings to surprise attack, loot, and vacate before anyone really knew what happened.

Lindisfarne Priory Viking stone, a 9th Century grave marker. 41

Lindisfarne was a defenseless place known as the "Holy Island." The viking raid on it caused much consternation throughout the Christian World and is most often marked as being the "official" beginning of the Viking Age.

This map shows the location of the Holy Island, Lindisfarne on the northeastern coast of Northumbria of the modern day UK Island. The raiding Norse had probably landed near the location from the sea and sailed up or down the coast until they spotted a location to attack.

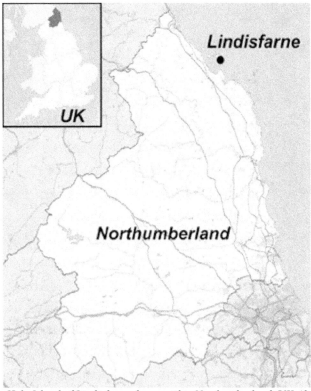

Holy Island of Lindisfarne shown within Northumberland, UK.43

The Viking Age is the period of time when the Norse are most often talked about. The Age when the Norse invaded much of Europe during a time when they became known as the Vikings.

The Viking Age is not the beginning of the Norse people or the start of their culture. The roots of the Norse go back even further. All the way back to the Megalithic and Neolithic Eras of the Stone Age.

The Stone age for the Norse was very different than what we were taught about the Stone Age in regards to other cultures. Other cultures such as the Mediterranean Cultures are where we gathered most of our information about the stone ages, the bronze age, and the iron ages of humankind in general. But the Norse people experienced the change of the Ages much differently than other cultures.

The Stone Ages, the Bronze (Copper) Age, and the Iron ages for the Norse progressed very different that that of the rest of the World. So different were the early stages of Nordic cultural evolution that they have their own separate categories and classifications for their cultural evolutionary eras. The culturally specific Norse classifications are labeled as: The Nordic Stone Age, The Nordic Bronze Age, and the Nordic Iron Age. The Nordic Iron Age is broken down into its own separate stages as well.

The Norse made the best of what they had available to them and with their unique regional situation, adapted with an uncanny sense of innovativeness. Their ability to trade and reach areas of trading to better improve their way of life was unmatched by any other culture in their day.

Nordic innovative technology that is still unmatched today. Their willingness to reach out far to other populations and cultures made them one of the most influential cultures out there.

Chapter 2
The Nordic Stone Age

From around the time during the Lower Paleolithic Era, which was about 1.8 million years ago, into the Upper Paleolithic Era, or 20,000 years ago; Europe was sparsely populated by Homo Erectus and Homo Neanderthalensis.

These were the ancient ancestors of modern humans. They were a hunter-gather type of people whom were eventually replaced by Homo Sapiens, modern humans.

Survival was hard and basic survival techniques were limited in an ever changing and unpredictable climate. The general practice of survival was to hunt and find whatever it was that they could scavenge to eat in order to survive. Hunting megafauna (large animals) was one of the most practiced means by groups that were able to survive in this environment.

To hunt these large animals, they had to develop ways to take them down. This included designing specialized tools such as spears and javelins to hunt.

Archeologists have found 380,000 year old wooden javelins belonging to these hunters in the Nordic Stone Age area. These javelins are the oldest complete hunting weapons ever found anywhere in the world and they were discovered in Schoningen, Germany.1

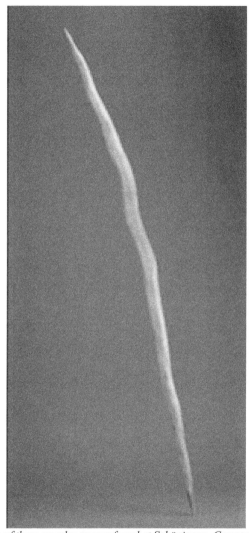

One of three wooden spears found at Schöningen, Germany.44

During the Upper Paleolithic to the Mesolithic Era, ranging from about 43,000 to 6,000 years ago, Europe's homo sapiens (human) hunter-gatherer populations gradually began to increase in number. During the last glacial maximum (Ice Age), much of Europe was depopulated because of the changed climate. After the thaw, Europe was then re-settled again approximately 15,000 years ago.

During this period of repopulation, groups of Europeans migrated long distances following the edge of the glacial ice in search of food. They were mostly hunting seals and following them along the edge of the ice and the sea. Some groups that were following seals and other marine food stuffs had made it all the way to North America traveling along the ice's edge that bridged across from Europe to North America.

We know that Stone Age Europeans had crossed over into North America during this time because several dozen European-style stone tools, dating back between 19,000 and 26,000 years, have been discovered at six different locations along the U. S. East Coast. What's more, chemical analysis carried out on a 19,000 year old stone knife found in Virginia, USA revealed that it was made of a French-originating flint.

That's a long distance for Stone Age people to travel, but it was necessary for their survival. They followed the food they were hunting in order to survive the exceptionally harsh climate.

What became of the Stone Aged Paleo-Europeans that had migrated to North America is still a puzzle for researchers to unravel. It is unclear as to whether or not they completely died out or if they attempted any form of settling. The most probable conclusion is that they continued to wander, hunting and searching for food until they eventually died out.

We do know Paleo-Europeans began entering the previously uninhabited North America at about the same time as the Paleo-Indians began crossing over via the Bering Sea land-bridge (Beringia). Similarly, Paleo-Indians followed game across the land-ice bridge much the same way as the Paleo-Europeans did on the opposite side of the continent.

As the glacial ice receded and the climate warmed up, the fauna that these stone aged hunter-gatherers hunted changed as some of the large herd animals began to become more scarce. There were fewer mammoth herds as the number of these animals began to dwindle.

Fortunately, the warmer climate brought new sources of meat, such as growing herds of reindeer, that had become more readily available over time. Eventually, reindeer became a main source of hide, bone, antler, and of course a primary source of meat.

It was during this time of the Nordic Stone Age that the Norse people existed as nomadic reindeer hunters. From 13,500 BC to 11,000 BC is a period of time during the Nordic Stone Age that is called the **Hamburg Culture**. This time period is classified by the shouldered spear and arrow points discovered that date to the period and zinken tools found that the Hamburg Culture people used as chisels when working with horns.

Also specific to the Hamburg Culture are the tanged Havelte-type arrow head points found which are described as being unique to the Hamburg Culture exclusively.

An illustration of a Hamburg Culture Arrow Head.2

Rock circles were also found in small settlements that are attributed to being used as weights to hold down the coverings of teepees. A teepee (also tepee and tipi) is a conical tent usually made of animal skins and supported by wooden poles. Teepees were used by primitive Nordic people just like the Great Plains Indians of North America and Saami people North of them in Scandinavia.

Within these sites were a great amount of

reindeer horn and bone remnants which shows that the reindeer were a very important prey. It appears that they lived in small groups that ranged from East of Poland to Northern France and Southern Scandinavia. It has also been discovered that they migrated along the Norwegian coast during the summer months because the sea level at the time was about 50 meters lower than it is today.

After this period in the late upper paleolithic age at around 11000 BC to 10000 BC came the **Ahrensburg Culture** with the complete extinction of megafauna, such as the mammoth. The ice began to recede in lower Sweden and Denmark from the Younger Dryas event (The Big Freeze) which caused much deforestation and there were land stretches exposed which are now under the North and Baltic Seas. This allowed these migrating hunter groups to reach areas by foot that later could only be reached by boats.

These Nordic nomads continued to hunt grazing wild reindeer and now had more incentive to exploit marine resources that became more accessible.

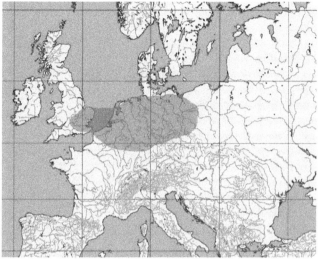

The Range of the Ahrensburg Culture. (Albin L. 2009)

The arrowheads of this time period changed to a shouldered, tanged point. This was a marked improvement in hunting methods as better tools were being made. With improved weapons and tools, hunters were able to hunt more proficiently and expand the variety of prey they hunted.

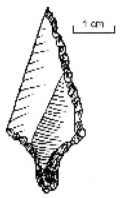

Drawing of an Ahrensburg Culture arrow head.3

Fish hooks have also been discovered, showing an improvement from relying on spear fishing by having the ability and knowledge to angle for fish. This may have contributed to a slowing in culture development, because the Neolithic Age (New Stone Age) is estimated to have begun around 5,000 BC in Northern Europe. This is about 4000 years after the Neolithic Age had already began in Southern Europe.

The **Linear Pottery culture** (Linearbandkeramik) was the next major archaeological horizon of the Northern European Neolithic Age happening at around 5500 BC to 4500 BC. This culture migrated less and began the gradual process of more permanently settling in areas. It was during the Linear Pottery culture that a trait started to co-evolve with the culture of dairy farming.

A significant change in lifestyle when agriculture began to develop with the keeping of livestock in lieu of complete dependency of hunting and gathering for survival. This was also a time where the transition from living a nomadic lifestyle in teepees to remaining in one place and living in more permanent structures such as communal long houses.

Excavations have revealed a large fortified settlement at Oslonki, Poland which dates to around 4300 BC that had nearly thirty trapezoidal longhouses located within in. The rectangular longhouses were between seven and forty-five meters long and were between five and seven meters wide. They were built with massive timber posts chinked with wattle and daub mortar.

Within them, and the nearly eighty grave sites on location, simple pottery items were found consisting of simple cups, bowls, vases, and jugs without handles. These pottery items were obviously designed as kitchen dishes and for transport and trade of food and liquids.

Linear Band Pottery.4

The use and life style associated with the Linear Band Pottery Culture began somewhat inland nearer other cultures and was most probably a learned concept from neighboring peoples to the South and East. The culture did not spread North or near the coastlines until later.

The culture that developed simultaneously to the North of the Linear Band Culture was the **Ertebølle culture**. This culture existed predominately in the Southern Areas of Scandinavia from about 5300 BC to 3950 BC.

These people were hunter-gatherers that

also relied on fishing and had some pottery making within their culture as well. This was about the time that this culture had some sparse transition to animal husbandry, such as cows and pigs.

They didn't practice cultivation yet, but they did trade for barley and emmer wheat (also known as farro or hulled wheat) from tribes south of them and engaged in seasonal cultivation of wild crops.

Map of European Middle Neolithic Period.5

By looking at the map above, you can see the proximity of the Western Linear Pottery cultures and the Ertebølle Cultures which encompass the majority of the Early Norse inhabited areas. This explains the trade exchanges and similarities between the cultures at that time. Their proximity and regular interaction with each other allowed exchanges in technology and ideas.

The climate became warmer than it is today in those regions and the water level soon became significantly higher. It was about five to six meters higher on the Baltic coastline than it is Today. Jutland (Denmark) was an archipelago during this time of small island chains and groups. The inland waters were rich with fish and the people living there flourished from this. They fished for these abundant marine life in their dugout canoes while also hunting whales and seals.

The materials they used were mostly made from wood, antler and bone as they lived in huts that were made of brush and light wood that was in abundance due to the warmer climate occurring during this time period.

This was along with having milder winters. Fire pits made from mud and clay were formed outside their huts. In these fore pits, they used firewood that was usually collected from the shorelines (dried drift wood) while they used dried fungus for tinder to help start their fires.

Evolving out of this culture was the **Funnelbeaker Culture** (Trichterbecherkultur) of around 4300 BC to 2800 BC. This culture is named for its characteristic ceramics with funnel-shaped tops which were probably used for drinking.

The people of this culture lived more inland in settlements that were located near those of the previous Ertebølle culture on the coast. They lived in single-family waffle and daub houses that were made from weaved lattice strips of wood or sticks and then 'daubed' with sticky material generally made from mud, clay, and straw mixtures.

The livelihood of these people relied on farming and animal husbandry which became their major sources of food. They raised sheep, cattle, pigs, and goats but also continued to rely on some hunting and fishing for food stuffs. They grew primitive wheat and barley on small patches, but these resources were fast depleted and still had not developed into a major dietary staple yet.

There was some small scale mining and collection of flint stone, which was traded into areas that lacked flint stone, such as the Scandinavian hinterlands. This culture also traded and imported copper items from Central Europe, especially tools, daggers, and axes.

During this time period a communal pile dwellings, also called stilt houses, were built and improved over several years by some communities that were only inhabited during the summer months. These buildings were used as social centers where clans gathered for festivities after the summer's hunting and harvesting season.

This may also have been an early concept of the Norse "Thing," where free men from different clans met to trade and negotiate disputes and make agreements. There were usually about 100 hearths made of limestone that were evenly distributed across the pile dwelling in huts that were supported by the many hazel stilts.

Around these limestone hearths, researchers found an abundance of residue from meals of charred wheat and barley, split and charred crab apples, hazel nut shells, and bone from cattle, sheep and pigs. There were also remains from game such as red deer, moose, wolf, and bear.

Additionally, researchers found remains from fowl such as mallard and black grouse and the remains of fish such as northern pike and perch. This shows how expanded their diets were becoming and the variety of meat consumed that they fished and hunted for.

The ceramics of these people were the same as those of the hunter-gatherer Pitted Ware culture, but the tools and weapons were the same as those of the Funnelbeaker culture. This shows a mixture of culture and technology shared between them.

The remains of craftsmanship were relatively few, suggesting that their tools were transported to the communal pile dwellings from the workshops where they lived the majority of the time. Meaning, they only came to the communal sites for short periods of time to trade and exchange ideas. Additionally meeting for religious rites and probably to make sacrifices to their gods.

Among the most remarkable finds in these communal sites were double edged battle axes, which appear to have played an important role in their culture as far as being symbols of status.

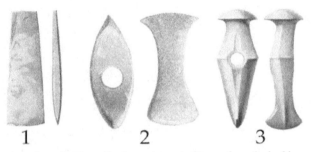

Axes from the Funnelbeaker culture. 1. thin-neck ax, 2. double-edged battle ax, 3. polygonal battle ax.6

During the time of these Nordic Stone Age cultures, a prevalence of a gene that allowed adults of Northern European descent to digest lactose originated and spread to other cultures to become virtually universal. This was a genetic variant that was either rare or completely absent in early farmers from Central Europe.

Lactase is an enzyme produced in the digestive system of infants and some (mostly European) adult humans to break down lactose. The lactase enzyme is essential in the digestion of whole milk. The absence of the lactase enzyme is what causes a person consuming dairy products to experience the symptoms of lactose intolerance. Ancient DNA extracted from three individuals belonging to the Funnelbeaker Culture in Gökhem, Sweden were found to possess these traits.

This genetic trait made cattle an even more important resource to the Norse than just that of meat and hide. The milk could now be regularly harvested for consumption, which later evolved into cheese, butter and other dairy products which became a very important part of their culture.

Evolving from this culture followed the **Battleaxe Culture**, also known as the **Boat-Ax Culture** or more accurately, the **Corded Ware Culture** of approximately 2800 BC that continued well into the Nordic Bronze Age that began around 1700 BC.

The name 'boat-ax' comes from the fact that the over 3000 battle axes found scattered throughout the Nordic areas of Scandinavia made from ground stone were shaped similar to that of boats.

Boat-shaped battle axes typical of the Battle Ax Culture.7

This time period has also been nicknamed the Age of Crushed Skulls by Swedish writer Herman Lindqvist. due to evidence of skull damage in grave sites caused by axes. This is also highly suggestive as to why the style of spangenhelm helmets worn by the Norse may have evolved to the distinctive conical shape as a means to protect the head from such blows.

The culture of this age gets its more accurate label as the Corded-Ware Culture, because of the change in pottery during this time period. Pottery that was highly influenced from pastoral societies on the Central European steppes.

Corded-Ware pottery from around 2500 BC.8

The span of Corded-Ware Culture coincides with the Funnel-Beaker Culture as improvements were learned from neighboring groups and a greater reliance on farming began to evolve. Much of the early distribution of this culture was more inland in its beginnings than from the coastal regions. The people of this culture shared many features of the Funnel-Beaker Culture such as use of horses and wheeled carts (which were possibly drawn by oxen) that originated from the European steppes.

The improvements from this culture spread quickly to other settlements due to the aforementioned higher sea levels which instead of being a hindrance and dividing the cultures, allowed them to use the dividing waterways and the seas as highways. This developed into a maritime culture that enhanced their geographical spread and economies with expanded trade.

Chapter 3
The Metallic Ages

The Norse "Metallic Ages," so called because they date the time periods when the Norse people are recorded to have been working with metals such as: copper, bronze, and iron.

This Age also includes the Migration Period (the Age of Heroes), because it happened during the time of the Germanic Iron Age when there were great southerly migrations of the Nordic people.

The Norse Metallic Ages are:

* The Nordic Bronze Age 1700 BC –500 BC.

* The Pre-Roman Iron Age 500 BC – 1 AD.

* The Roman Iron Age 1 AD - 400 AD.

* The Germanic Iron Age 400 AD – 800 AD.

* The Migration Period ("The Heroic Age") 400 - 800 AD.

The **Nordic Bronze Age**, also called the Northern Bronze Age, occurred approximately 1700 BC through 500 BC. The Scandinavian Norse joined the European Bronze Age relatively late and began from importing goods such as European bronze and gold items by means of trade.

During this time many rock carvings depicting ships began showing up, along with the early burial custom of making monument "Stone Ship" burial mounds. These Stone Ships varied in size from small to huge and were generally around other burial grounds and religious ceremonial locations. It is believed that the building of these ships, along with equipping the bereaved with other items, would help them along in their journey to underworld of Hel.

Two Stone Ships (Burial Grounds).9

There wasn't a written language developed during this Age yet and most stone carvings depicted either ships or elk. The stones are dated in comparison with bronze axes and swords found from the same era.

Also marking the Nordic Bronze Age was the fact that there was a warmer climate in the region similar to that of Northern France today due to climate change that happened around 2700 BC. This allowed Norse communities to live closer together in denser populations as they experienced better farming conditions. Grapes were even grown in parts of Scandinavia during this time.

This did change because during the end of the Norse Bronze Age, from around 850 BC through 650 BC, the climate changed again becoming colder and wetter which dramatically altered living conditions and southerly migrations began.

The Norse then developed into what's called the **Pre-Roman Iron Age** that ranged from around 500 BC through until the 1st century BC when they came into contact with the Romans. This time line is the earliest part of the Nordic Iron Age that occurred in Norse inhabited areas where a wealth of archaeological artifacts have surfaced leading scholars to believe that Pre-Roman Iron Age Norse evolved without completely making a transition out of the Nordic Bronze age.

Although the use of iron began to increase, bronze was still mostly used during this time. The Norse use of iron gradually increased with strong Celtic influences until greater contact with the Romans in the 1st century BC, when Nordic use of Iron became even more influenced by Roman culture.

It was during this period of the Nordic Pre-Iron age before 71 BC, that many Norse came down to unite with a Germanic leader by the name of Ariovistus. Ariovistus had promised the Norse lands for resettlement in Gallic areas as reward for joining his army and fighting for him.

Ariovistus is described by Julius Caesar's firsthand account of the Gallic Wars, as rex Germanorum (King of Germania), even though Germania wasn't united under a single King. The Celtic/Gallic Sequani People asked Ariovistus for assistance in their war against their hereditary rivals, the Gallic Aedui. The Aedui people were aligned with the Romans and the Sequani were in need of assistance in their war against them. Ariovistus seen this as an opportunity for expansion.

Ariovistus, with an army built up from various Germanic and Norse tribes, came to the assistance of the Sequani and defeated the Aedui. However, the Sequani people ended up worse off then before and had lost a third of their lands that were seized by Ariovistus, whom threatened to take a third more because he had to make room and provide the promised settlements for the approximate 24,000 Norse Harudes that had come to assist him from the North. He had also subjugated the Sequani people he had come to help into semi slavery.

The Harudes (or Charudes) were the Norse/Germanic group first mentioned by Julius Caesar as one of the tribes whom had joined Ariovistus crossing the Rhine River to battle the Gallic Aedui. The Norse Harudes had gathered in Jutland (Denmark Today) from the North in Scandinavia and then came South to join with the Germanic tribes that were forming. Their name suggests that they may have come from Hardanger region in the county of Hordaland, Norway and sailed to Jutland.

The Sequani, whom had asked Ariovistus for help but became subjugated and lost their lands in doing so, appealed to their previous enemies the Romans for help now. Julius Caesar came to their aid and drove back the Germanic and Norse tribesmen across the Rhine in 58 BC. However afterward, various tribesmen continued opportunistic raids on Gaul.

They would cross the Rhine to raid and then afterwards sought refuge from retaliation by crossing back to the eastern side of the Rhine. This pushed Caesar to build a bridge to cross the Rhine and confront the opportunistic raiders and to show support for the Germanic tribe, the Ubians that were also allied with the Romans.

The first bridge Caesar had built in 58 BC, was built with a Legion of 40,000 troops in ten days. He crossed his army into Germania and burnt down some villages, but the tribes had moved eastward and converged together to meet Caesar's army in force. Caesar had heard of this plan and crossed back over the Rhine into Gaul and took the bridge down with him. He had only been in the area for 18 days.

In 55 BC, Caesar came again with his army and built a new bridge within a few days and again crossed the Rhine. However, the tribes retreated so Caesar returned back into Gaul and took his second bridge down as he did so. Caesar had displayed to the Norse and Germanic tribes that the Rhine wasn't a natural obstacle that would provide them with security from the Romans, as Rome could cross the river at any time they wished.

This act secured the eastern front of Gaul, which later had built permanent bridges for trade with allied Germanic tribes that sought out the stability that Rome offered.

This was during the time period known in the Nordic Iron Ages as the **Roman Iron Age**, which ran from around 1 BC to 400 AD, when the Roman Empire had the greatest hold and influence over the Germanic tribes to the north of their empire. An Roman influence that reached all the way into Scandinavia, as climate change continued to push many Norse south to seek places for resettlement.

This was also a time when a great amount of imported goods spread throughout Scandinavia that originated from the Roman Empire such as coins, glass beakers, bronze and iron items such as weapons and other objects. More gold and silver came into Nordic regions towards the end of the Roman Iron Age when Rome began to falter and were ransacked more often by neighboring Germanic tribes.

At the end of the Roman Iron Age, cultural change began happening in Norse areas that was again also influenced by climatic changes that had caused dramatic changes in the flora and fauna. This period in Scandinavia is called the "**Findless Age**" due to the lack of archaeological finds resulting from the scarcity of populations in the area that left behind few traces of their presence. The deteriorating climate pushed Norse populations south as they sought better more arable lands.

This "findless" time period is called the **Migration Age** which happened at the same time as the **Germanic Iron Age** that occurred from 400 AD to 800 AD.

It is a time period that is also called the "Heroic Age" and the period of "Barbarian Invasions," because of the consequence of Norse southerly migrations that encroached into the lands of other tribes that were already present.

This Nordic incursion caused much friction between pre-existing populations and resulted in many battles and wars. The result of some of these many battles became Sagas about warrior heroes – making it the Heroic Age.

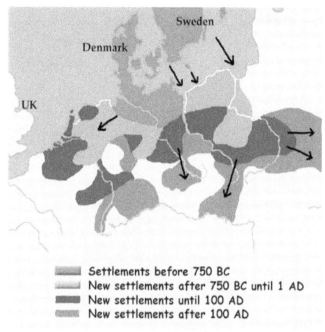

Settlements before 750 BC
New settlements after 750 BC until 1 AD
New settlements until 100 AD
New settlements after 100 AD

The expansion of the Norse and Germanic tribes 750 BC– 100 AD.

The waning of the once powerful Roman Empire and the growing Celtic and Germanic Kingdoms led to an increase in gold flowing in the north resulting in many works of gold as the Norse used it to make decorative ornaments. After Rome fell, gold then became scarce in the northern regions and the Norse began to use gilded bronze once again.

The Nordic Migration Period happened in two phases. The first phase happening between 300 AD to 500 AD, which put control of the then Western Roman Empire into the hands of the Germanic people.

The second phase of migrations took place 500 AD through 700 AD with settlements expanding into Central and Eastern Europe. This expansion spread all the way into the Lombardy region of Northern Italy.

There is some dispute as to whether this age should be called the Migration Period or the Invasion Period. As there are several explanations as to why the sudden and heavy appearance of 'barbarians' on the Roman frontiers. Climate change pushing populations south into more fertile croplands and the effect of tribes coming in from every direction pushing one people into another, causing a 'domino-effect.'

It's also seen that the increased barbarian and Norse movements into formerly controlled Roman lands are the result of a falling Rome, not the cause.

References

1. Kouwenhoven, Arlette P. "World's Oldest Spears." Archaeological Institute of America. Volume 50 Number 3, May/June 1997.
2. A drawing of a point from the paleolithic Hamburg culture arrow head. Drawing by Micke. 2007.
3. Drawing of a Ahrensburg point, Germany. José-Manuel Benito. August 2006.
4. Linear Band Pottery, Collection University of Jena, Bereich für Ur- und Frühgeschichte an der Friedrich-Schiller-Universität Jena. Photo by Roman Grabolle. January 2005.
5. Map of European Middle Neolithic Period. Created by Joostik. December 2012.
6. Tunnackigyxa (thin-neck axe), from Skåne. 1st (1876–1899), 2nd (1904–1926) or 3rd (1923–1937) edition of Nordisk familjebok.
7. Boat-shaped battle axes typical of the Battle Axe Culture. Pottery vessels and axes, chisels and arrows made of flint were also common. The National Museum of Denmark. 2013.
8. Corded ware pottery from around 2500 BC in the Museum für Vor- und Frühgeschichte (Museum of prehistory and early history), Berlin. Photo by Einsamer Schütze. June 2011.
9. Two of the viking stone ships (burial grounds) at Badelunda near Västerås, Sweden. Photo by: "Berig." 1 May 2005.
10. A modern version of England 878 AD made using Inkscape by Hel-hama. 13 June 2012.

11. The approximate extent of Old Norse and related languages in the early 10th century. Created by Wiglaf, based on Europe plain rivers by Dbachmann. 20 April 2005.

12. Gwyn Jones. A History of the Vikings. Oxford: Oxford University Press. 1968. p. 177.

13. Ian Riddler. Two Late Saxon Combs from the Longmarket Excavations. Canterbury's Archaeology 1989/1990, The 14th Annual Report of Canterbury Archaeological Trust Ltd.

14. Reconstruction of the Køstrup apron-dress at the National Museum of Denmark. Photo by Hilde Thunem

15. Wikinger Museum Foteviken auf Skanör. Wikinger (Guide in Wikingerkleidung) Wolfgang Sauber. 17 August 2007.

16. Germanic thing, drawn after the depiction in a relief of the Column of Marcus Aurelius (AD 193)

17. Egill Skallagrímsson engaging in holmgang with Berg-Önundr, painting by Johannes Flintoe (1787–1870)

18. Fig. 885. Drawing of a Shield from Gokstad ship. CH 6, pg 98. "The Viking Age" vol. 1 by Paul B Du Chaillu. 1889.

19. Modern reconstructions of Viking shield. Danish National Museum. Photo: Jacob Nyborg Andreassen. Accessed online 2013.

20. Viking "bearded axe" blade 1000 AD (top), and a German horseman's axe blade 1100 AD (bottom). Incitatus. 4 December 2006.

21. Replica Danish ax head. Forged by Bronze Lion. 14 August 2008.

22. Infantry armed with spears, swords and battle axes that fought the huscarls Harold Hastings. Bayeux Tapestry, Bayeux. Picture by Urban, February 2005.

23. Viking Spearheads. The Vikings (Pelican Books ISBN 10: 0140204598 / ISBN 13: 9780140204599) by Brondsted, Johannes. 1960.

24. From Njáls saga: Gunnar fights his ambushers at Rangá. Illustration from "Vore fædres liv" : karakterer og skildringer fra sagatiden / samlet og udggivet af Nordahl Rolfsen ; oversættelsen ved Gerhard Gran., Kristiania: Stenersen,

1898.

25. Ulfberth sword found in Finland at the National Museum in Copenhagen, Denmark (Historisk Viden, Danmark). 2013 online.

26. Example of pattern forged sword at the National Museum in Copenhagen, Denmark (Historisk Viden, Danmark). 2013 online.

27. Thorsberg moor, Germany find. Fig. 412. Brynja or coat of chain mail, 3 feet long. CH 12. pg 215. "The Viking Age" vol 2 by Paul B Du Chaillu. 1889.

28. Chainmail sample from the mail shirt found in Gjermundbu, Norway. Universitets Oldsaksamling in Oslo, Norway. Accessed 2013.

29. Viking warrior with leather lamellar armour. Via Elettra Gardini www.pinterest.com 2013. Note: the original source of this picture is of yet to be found. It was used in 'fair use' as the best example of replicated lamellar armor in use to educate the reader in their research on Viking armor.

30. Viking helmet from the Gjermundbu gravesite now in the Museum of Cultural History, University of Oslo. Photo: NTNU Museum February 10, 2010.

31. Replica Conical Spangenhelm with nasal made from 16 gauge steel by Royal Oak Armoury Artisan Crafts / Metal Work. Photo taken by Royal Oak Armoury on June 15, 2012.

32. Gokstadskipet, Vikingskipmuseet, Oslo. Photo by Karamell 2005.

33. Iceland spar, perhaps the medieval sunstone. Decemeber 2010 by ArniEin.

34. A Sami indigenous northern European family in Norway around 1900. The picture was probably taken in 1896 by an unknown author.

35. Nordic Sami (Saami) people in Sapmi (Lapland) in front of two Lavvo Tents. Photo taken 1900-1920 by Granbergs Nya Aktiebolag.

36. A young Oglala girl sitting in front of a tipi, with a puppy beside her, probably on or near Pine Ridge Reservation. Photo taken 1891 by John C. H. Grabill.

37. *Sioux Teepees. Watercolor on paper by Karl Bodmer from his travel to the U.S. 1832-1834.*
38. *Christian Krohg: Illustration for Olav Tryggvasons saga, Heimskringla 1899.*
39. *Hamilton, Hugo. 1830. Sketches of Scandinavia's ancient history. Stockholm: Gjöthström & Magnusson.*
40. *"The destruction of Irminsul by Charlemagne" (1882) by Heinrich Leutemann. - Wägner, William. 1882. Nordic-Germanic gods and heroes. Otto Spamer, Leipzig and Berlin. Page 159.*
41. *Lindisfarne Priory Viking stone, a 9th Century grave marker with seven warriors carved into the surface. Holy Island, Northumberland.*
42. *Statue of a Viking in Gimli, Manitoba (Canada). Photo by Magickallwiz, 2008.*
43. *Lindisfarne shown within Northumberland. Northumberland UK location map by Nilfanion, 2010.*
44. *One of three wooden spears found at Schöningen, Germany. Photo by: Chip Clark, Smithsonian Institution. 1995.*
45. *John Cassell. 19th century depiction of a Pict. John Cassell's Illustrated History of England: volume 1 From the earliest period to the reign of Edward the Fourth. Cassell, Petter & Galpin. 1865.*
46. *The Danish Ship called the Raven, Viking Ship, Pre-800 AD. Historical archives of LIFE Magazine.*
47. *"King Rorik" by Hermanus Willem Koekkoek (1867–1929) Teutonic Myth and Legend by Donald A. MacKenzie, London, Gresham Publications. 1912.*
48. *King Ælla of Northumbria's execution of Ragnar Lodbrok. Hamilton, Hugo. 1830. Teckningar ur Skandinaviens Äldre Historia. Stockholm: Gjöthström & Magnusson.*
49. *Peter Nicolai Arbo. Battle of Stamford Bridge. December 31, 1869.*
50. *A battle between 'Anglo-Saxons' and 'Vikings'. Staged by 're-enactors.' Source: bbc.co.uk.*

51. King of Mercia Athelred seen on the exterior of Lichfield Cathedral.

52. Reenactors depicting King Alfred with the West Saxon (Wessox) forces battling the Danish Norsemen of the Great Summer Army.

53. Statue of King Alfred at Wantage created by DJ Clayworth. 2004.

54. Statue of the first King of Norway, Harald Hårfagre (Fairhair). Made by Einar Jónsson in 1924 and located on Arnarhóll, Reykjavík.

55. Viking Ships besieging Paris. Der Spiegel Geschichte (6/2010): The Vikings - Warriors culture: The life of the Northmen. Spiegel-Verlag Rudolf Augstein GmbH & Co. KG, Hamburg 2010, p.33

56. Portrait of Charles the Bald (823-877) at Palace of Versailles, France.

57. A map of the routes taken by the Great Heathen Army from 865 to 878 based on Stenton 'Anglo-Saxon England' chapter 8 and Hill ' An Atlas of Anglo-Saxon England' p40-1. by Hel-hama. June 26, 2012.

58. Map of the Duchy of Normandy.

59. Portrait of Robert I of Western Francia, King of the Franks.

60. British Isles in 10th century represented with the coastline at the time. Created by Ikonact. August 31, 2013.

61. Rollo statue depicted among the 6 dukes of Normandy in the town square of Falaise.

62. Silver penny of Eric Bloodaxe. A coin of the last Viking King of York, Northumbria. It circulated during the Viking Age at 947 to 954 AD. British Museum.

63. Raven's Banner (hrafnsmerki) as used by Jarl Sigurd.

64. Erik the Red statue at Qagssiarssuk, Greenland.

65. Leif Erikson statue in front of Hallgrimskirkja.Iceland.

66. A depiction of the death of Thorvald Eriksson which took place somewhere in North America in 1004 AD. Did the Vikings Beat the Pilgrims to Plymouth? By Patrick Browne. July 24, 2014

67. *Death of Ymir. Lorenz Frølich (25 October 1820 – 25 October 1908).*
68. *Illustration of Auðumbla licking Búri out of a salty ice-block, from an Icelandic 18th century manuscript by Jakob Sigurðsson.(1765-1766).*
69. *Two dwarfs as depicted in the Poetic Edda poem Völuspá by Lorenz Frølich. 1895.*
70. *"The Wolves Pursuing Sol and Mani." J.C. Dollman. 1909.*
71. *Scultpure of the first living people, Ask and Embla, at the main square in Sölvesborg, Sweden.*
72. *Artist's depiction of Yggdrasil and the nine realms.*
73. *Odin the Wanderer by George von Rosen. 1896.*
74. *Odin sits atop his steed Sleipnir, his ravens Huginn and Muninn and wolves Geri and Freki nearby by Lorenz Frølich. 1895.*
75. *Odin Hanging on the World Tree. Illustration for Die Edda: Germanische Götter und Heldensagen by Hans von Wolzogen. 1920.*
76. *"Frigg and Odin in Grímnismál by Frølich" by Lorenz Frølich. Published in Gjellerup, Karl.1895.*
77. *Statute of Balder. Sculpted by Bengt Erland Fogelberg. 1842.*
78. *Artist depiction of Thor Odinsson with Toothgrinder and Toothgnasher. mytholipedia.com. 2014.*
79. *Drawing of silver amulet representing Mjöllnir, the hammer of Thor. Discovered in Skåne, Sweden.1877.*
80. *Artist's depiction of the Tyr, God of War.*
81. *The Battle of Thor with the serpent of Midgard. Painted by Henry Fuseli. Royal Academy of Arts, London. 1788.*
82. *Artist's depiction of the Symbol of Jörmungandr, The Midgard Serpent.*
83. *"The Punishment of Loki", by Louis Huard. The Heroes of Asgard: Tales from Scandinavian Mythology by A & E Keary. MacMillan & Co, London. 1891.*
84. *The Norse god Heimdallr blowing the horn Gjallarhorn by Lorenz Frølich (1820-1908).*

85. "The goddess Sif" by John Charles Dollman. Myths of the Norsemen from the Eddas and Sagas by Guerber, H. A.. London. 1909.

86. "Hermod before Hela" by John Charles Dollman. Myths of the Norsemen from the Eddas and Sagas by Guerber, H. A.. London. 1909.

87. The god Freyr by Johannes Gehrts. 1901.

88. "Kampf der untergehenden Götter" by Friedrich Wilhelm Heine.1882.

89. Njord's desire of the Sea by W. G. Collingwood. 1908.

90. Skadi's longing for the Mountains by W. G. Collingwood. 1908.

91. Týr and Fenrir by John Bauer. 1911.

92. Hel by Johannes Gehrts. 1889.

93. An illustration of Lifþrasir and Líf by Lorenz Frølich.Published in Den ældre Eddas Gudesange by Gjellerup, Karl. 1895.

94. The battle between Surtr and Freyr at Ragnarök, illustration by Lorenz Frølich. Published in Den ældre Eddas Gudesange by Gjellerup, Karl. 1895.

95. The Sutton Hoo helmet located at the British Museum. 2011.

96. Replica of Viking Era Merchant Knarr. Published in Mobility, the Viking Way. By Alan Robert Lancaster. March 28, 2015.

CPSIA information can be obtained
at www.ICGtesting.com
Printed in the USA
LVHW081530250319
611739LV00043B/1154/P